STATUS AND TRENDS OF WETLANDS

IN THE COASTAL WATERSHEDS OF THE EASTERN UNITED STATES

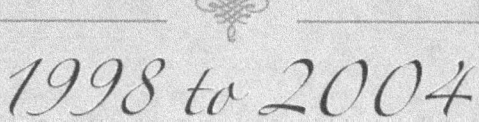

1998 to 2004

National Oceanic and Atmospheric Administration
National Marine Fisheries Service

and

U.S. Department of the Interior
Fish and Wildlife Service

STATUS AND TRENDS OF WETLANDS

COASTAL WATERSHEDS OF THE EASTERN UNITED STATES

1998 to 2004

Susan-Marie Stedman
NOAA, National Marine Fisheries Service
and
Thomas E. Dahl
U.S. Fish and Wildlife Service

ACKNOWLEDGMENTS

The authors wish to thank numerous agencies and individuals who provided input to this report. Particularly helpful were interagency briefings sponsored by the National Oceanic and Atmospheric Administration's (NOAA) National Marine Fisheries Service (NMFS) and the U.S. Environmental Protection Agency (EPA), Office of Wetlands, Oceans, and Watersheds, and attended by senior staff from the Council on Environmental Quality, Office of Management and Budget, U.S. Army Corps of Engineers, U.S. Department of Agriculture, NOAA, EPA, and U.S. Fish and Wildlife Service (FWS). These briefings helped formulate the context and presentation of the report findings and set the stage for additional collaborative efforts.

In addition, expert subject matter peer review was provided by the following technical specialists: Michael Scozzafava, Wetlands Division, EPA; William B. Ainslie, Wetlands Regulatory Section, EPA Region IV; Jennifer A. Wheeler, Waterbird Coordinator, Division of Migratory Bird Management, FWS; Martin Kodis, Chief, Branch of Resource and Mapping Support, Division of Habitat and Resource Conservation, FWS; FWS Regional Wetlands Coordinators Bill Kirchner, Brian Huberty, John Swords, Ralph Tiner, Kevin Bon, and Jerry Tande; Gary Whelan, Michigan Department of Natural Resources; and Tom Bigford, NMFS Office of Habitat Conservation.

CONTENTS

LIST OF FIGURES

LIST OF TABLES

EXECUTIVE SUMMARY

he National Oceanic and Atmospheric Administration's National Marine Fisheries Service, in cooperation with the U.S. Fish and Wildlife Service, analyzed the status and recent trends of wetland acreage in the coastal watersheds of the United States adjacent to the Atlantic Ocean, Gulf of Mexico, and Great Lakes. Sample plots were analyzed using digital high-resolution imagery to identify wetlands and land use changes observed between 1998 and 2004.

Results indicate that there were an estimated 39.8 million acres (16.1 million ha) of wetlands in these coastal watersheds in 2004. This represented 38 percent of the estimated total wetland acreage of 107.7 million acres (43.6 million ha) found in the conterminous United States.

Coastal watersheds experienced a net loss in wetland area. There was an estimated wetland loss of 361,000 acres (146,200 ha) in the coastal watersheds of the eastern U.S. between 1998 and 2004. This equated to an average annual net loss of about 59,000 acres (24,300 ha) over the 6-year period of this study. Gulf of Mexico coastal watersheds exhibited substantial losses in freshwater wetlands. This rate of loss was 6 times higher than the rate of freshwater vegetated wetlands losses in the Atlantic coastal watersheds. The estimated losses for all wetland types in the Gulf of

Mexico were 25 times higher than those estimates for the Atlantic over the course of this study. There was a net gain of an estimated 24,650 acres (10,000 ha) in the Great Lakes coastal watersheds over the same period of time.

In the time period encompassed by this study, trends suggested the country as a whole was gaining wetlands. From 1998 to 2004, wetland gains in the conterminous United States were estimated to have been 32,000 acres (12,960 ha) annually. The fact that coastal watersheds were losing wetlands despite the national trend of net gains points to the need for more research on the natural and human forces behind these trends and to an expanded effort on conservation of wetlands in these coastal areas. This point was highlighted in a 2008 report on wetland conservation by the Council on Environmental Quality. ▪

INTRODUCTION

his report is the result of a cooperative effort between the National Oceanic and Atmospheric Administration's (NOAA) National Marine Fisheries Service (NMFS) and the U.S. Fish and Wildlife Service (FWS). The efforts to monitor coastal wetland status and trends described in this report have been enhanced by the multi-agency involvement in the study's design, data collection, verification, and peer review of the findings.

NMFS' mission is to conserve, protect, and manage living marine resources in a way that ensures their continuation as functioning components of marine ecosystems, affords economic opportunities, and enhances the quality of life for the American public. Coastal wetlands provide valuable habitat for the vast majority of commercially harvested and recreational marine species. NOAA has produced regional and localized studies tracking land use and wetland change in coastal areas, as well as studies on the ecological and economic importance of coastal wetlands (NOAA 2005, 2008). The NMFS Habitat Program places special emphasis on the conservation of wetlands as essential fish habitat for harvested species and vital habitat for other species of ecological significance.

The mission of FWS is to conserve, protect, and enhance fish and wildlife and their habitats for the continuing benefit of the American people. The importance of wetlands as fish and wildlife habitat has always been the primary focus of FWS' wetland activities. FWS communicates information essential for public awareness and understanding of the importance of fish and wildlife resources and changes in environmental conditions that can affect the welfare of Americans. To this end, FWS maintains an active role in monitoring wetland habitats of the nation. NMFS and FWS have collaborated in a number of efforts that produce information on coastal habitats for fish and wildlife species. NOAA provided financial and logistical support for the previous two iterations of the Wetland Status and Trends report published in 2001 and 2006.

Because wetlands are often viewed as transitional habitats between water and dry land, wetland abundance, type, and quality are directly reflected in the health and abundance of many fish and wildlife species. Coastal wetland ecosystems include the wetlands immediately along the sea coast or Great Lakes and along the rivers and bays that make up the coastal drainage area. Coastal wetlands support life on land and in the sea by providing nutrients, food, and places for plants and animals to reproduce and grow.

The Emergency Wetlands Resources Act of 1986 (Public Law 99-645) was enacted to promote the conservation of our nation's wetlands. The Act requires FWS to conduct wetland status and trend studies of the nation's wetlands at periodic intervals. This is accomplished using a stratified, random sampling design where sample plots are examined with the use of remotely sensed imagery, in combination with field work, to determine wetland change.

The most recent national study detailed the status and trends of wetlands from 1998 to 2004 (Dahl 2006). Wetland trends data collected as part of that effort also provided statistical estimates of wetland status and trends for the coastal watersheds contained in this report. This report analyzed 2,265 sample plots using digital high-resolution imagery to identify wetlands, deepwater habitats, and uplands. Changes in areal extent or type of wetland observed in the sample plots between 1998 and 2004 were recorded. Field verification was completed for 824 of the sample plots (36 percent).

This report presents the latest status information on coastal wetland resources and provides estimates of losses or gains that occurred in the coastal watersheds between 1998 and 2004. These data were analyzed beyond the national data set and provide new information about wetland trends specific to the coastal watersheds of the Atlantic, Gulf of Mexico, and Great Lakes coasts It should be noted that the estimates of wetland area were made prior to hurricanes Katrina and Rita in 2005. ■

COASTAL WETLANDS

Coastal wetlands occur along the shores of the United States, with the largest expanses along the Gulf of Mexico and southern Atlantic coasts. Coastal wetland ecosystems are integrated by the water that flows through them, which connects the wetlands immediately along the ocean or Great Lakes with those of the rivers and floodplains upstream. Coastal wetland types are as diverse as salt marshes, bottomland hardwood swamps, fresh marshes, mangrove swamps, and shrub depressions known in the southeast United States as "pocosins." The definitive factor in coastal wetlands is the effect of tides on the watershed as a whole. For this reason, coastal wetlands can be described as all wetlands below head of tide in watersheds that drain to the Atlantic Ocean, Gulf of Mexico, or Pacific Ocean, as well as wetlands that drain directly to one of the Great Lakes. The target population of wetlands included in this study was all wetlands in the coastal watersheds of the Atlantic, Gulf of Mexico, and Great Lakes.[1]

Coastal wetlands, like inland wetlands, are among the most productive ecosystems on Earth. The bidirectional water movement caused by tides in marine coastal wetlands can augment productivity to even higher levels in what is called a "tidal subsidy." The close connection between coastal wetlands and large water bodies provides extensive coastal transport mechanisms driven by littoral drift and larger ocean currents such as the Gulf Stream, and the large interlake circulation cells exhibited by each of the Great Lakes can magnify the role coastal wetlands play on marine ecosystems. More than half of commercially harvested fish in the United States depend on estuaries and nearby coastal waters at some stage in their life cycle (Lellis-Dibble et al. 2008). Coastal habitats provide spawning grounds, nurseries, shelter, and food for finfish, shellfish, birds, and other wildlife (NRC 1997). The abundance and health of adult stocks of commercially harvested shrimp, blue crabs, oysters, and other species are directly related to wetland quality and quantity (Turner and Boesch 1988; Stedman and Hanson 2000). The nation's coastal resources also provide resting, feeding, and breeding habitat for 85 percent of waterfowl and other migratory birds (EPA 2005), and nearly 45 percent of the nation's endangered and threatened species are dependent on coastal habitats (FWS 1995). Wetlands help improve surface water quality by filtering, storing, and detoxifying residential, agricultural, and urban wastes, and can buffer coastal areas against storm and wave damage and help stabilize shorelines. The economic value of coastal habitats is likely to be in the hundreds of billions of dollars, if not more (Pendleton 2008).

Because of their close proximity to terrestrial systems, coastal wetlands are vulnerable to land development, pollutant discharges, and other human activities. Coastal wetland losses and degradation can be directly traced to population pressures and other human-induced changes occurring along the coast. Expanding populations place pressures on existing natural resources, particularly wetlands, which are vulnerable to changes in water flow, pollution, and habitat fragmentation. Human populations in coastal areas have increased steadily since 1970 (U.S. Commission on Ocean Policy 2004). Currently over half the population of the United States lives in coastal counties at densities about five times greater than those of non-coastal counties (Crossett et al. 2004). This trend of people moving to coastal areas is expected to continue in the coming decades.

The results of previous studies of coastal wetland status and trends are summarized in Table 1. Understanding the status and trends of coastal wetlands is complicated, in part, by the lack of a universally accepted definition

---

[1] This study did not include the Pacific coast due to insufficient data.

of "coastal" in past studies. NOAA produced two estimates of coastal wetlands: one used state data for wetlands in coastal counties in the Atlantic, Pacific, and Gulf of Mexico coasts (Alexander et al. 1986), and the other used a statistical sampling of the existing FWS National Wetlands Inventory maps for wetlands in coastal counties and watersheds along the Atlantic, Pacific, and Gulf of Mexico coasts (Field et al. 1991).

The two estimates of wetland area generated by these studies differed substantially, although the relative abundance of wetlands along the Gulf of Mexico and relatively small amount of wetlands on the Pacific coast were consistent between the two studies. The study by Field et al. (1991) estimated that about a third of the country's wetlands were coastal.

TABLE 1. Previous Studies of Coastal Wetland Status and Trends (Atlantic, Pacific, and Gulf of Mexico only)					
Study	Coastal Definition	Year	Area Estimate (acres)	Time Period	Loss Estimate (acres/year)
Gosselink and Bauman 1980	non-fresh tidal wetlands in coastal counties	1922	9,980,000		
		1954	9,330,000	1922 – 1954	20,000
		1974	8,405,000	1954 – 1974	46,000
Alexander et al. 1986	wetlands in coastal counties	1970s	11,000,000		NA
Tiner 1991	estuarine wetlands (excluding the Pacific coast)	1970s	5,532,000	1974-1983	7,900
Field et al. 1991	wetlands in coastal watersheds	1980s	27,000,000		NA
Brady and Flather 1994	tidal wetlands on non-federal lands	1982	6,713,460	1982-1987	19,323
		1987	6,617,380		
Brady and Goebel 2002	wetlands in coastal counties on non-federal lands	1992	22,430,000	1992-1997	24,400
		1997	22,300,000		

In 1994, scientists with the U.S. Department of Agriculture's (USDA) Natural Resources Conservation Service reviewed the USDA's Natural Resources Inventory (NRI) data for 1982 to 1987 and separated it into "coastal" and "inland" using the definitions in the FWS' original wetland classification system known as "Circular 39" (Brady and Flather 1994). They updated the work in 2002 (Brady and Goebel 2002) for the 1992 to 1997 data, including all wetlands in coastal counties as coastal wetlands. Like the NOAA estimates, this included only the Atlantic, Pacific, and Gulf of Mexico coasts of the coterminous United States. The 2002 results are close to those of the second NOAA inventory

in that approximately a third of the wetlands in the coterminous United States were found to be "coastal," with the majority of them in the freshwater system.

Again, lack of consistency in defining the term and geographical extent of "coastal" has hampered interpretation of the above studies. Dahl (2006) pointed out that geographic dissimilarity, differences in terminology, and different time periods accounted for discrepancies in wetland loss estimates in Louisiana. Gosselink and Baumann (1980) compiled information from the USDA's swamplands survey of 1922, the first National Wetlands Inventory in 1954 (Shaw and Fredine

1956), and state surveys made in the early 1970s for the Atlantic, Pacific, and Gulf of Mexico coasts of the coterminous United States. They calculated two coastal wetland loss rates: 19,000 acres per year for 1922–1954 and 46,000 acres per year for 1954–1974. The two studies using NRI data yielded estimates of 19,000 acres per year for 1982–1987 and 32,600 acres per year for 1992–1997. However, it is important to remember that none of these studies, not even the two using NRI data, used consistent methodologies, so these rates are not comparable and can be used only as estimates of the order of magnitude of coastal wetland loss during those periods.

Brady and Goebel (2002) drew some interesting conclusions from the 1992–1997 data analysis. They stated that coastal counties (excluding the Great Lakes) occupy 7 percent of the land area, have 20 percent of the wetlands, and 31 percent of the gross wetland loss (on non-federal, rural lands). They also found that 42 percent of the loss of wetlands to development occurred in coastal counties, and that wetland gains in inland counties nearly offset losses, whereas the area of wetlands lost in coastal counties was more than four times the area of wetlands gained.[2] These results pointed to the need for a more in-depth and consistent approach to understand the current status and trends of coastal wetlands. ■

---

[2] This study made no attempt to determine the quality of wetlands that were lost or gained.

CURRENT STUDY AREA, PROCEDURES, AND OBJECTIVES

Analysis of the FWS' national wetlands status and trends dataset was conducted to provide information specifically on the status and extent of wetland resources in the coastal watersheds of the Atlantic, Gulf of Mexico, and Great Lakes (Figure 1). The most recent national study detailed the status and trends of wetlands from 1998 to 2004 (Dahl 2006). In that study, 4,682 randomly selected plots were assessed using digital high-resolution imagery to identify change in wetlands, deepwater habitats, and uplands. Each sample plot was 4.0 square miles total area (2,560 acres). For each plot, digital aerial imagery was acquired and interpreted to identify wetlands, deepwater habitats, and uplands and the changes in areal extent or type of wetland observed in the sample plots between 1998 and 2004. This report presents additional information specific to the coastal watersheds areas of the Atlantic, Gulf or Mexico, and Great Lakes coasts. Findings were based on 2,265 sample plots that fell within the coastal watershed study area.

Figure 1. Coastal watersheds of the Atlantic, Gulf of Mexico, and Great Lakes.

The United States has been divided and subdivided into successively smaller hydrologic units, which have been classified into four levels by the U.S. Geological Survey (Seaber et al. 1994).

Since approximately 1990, NOAA has used a specific methodology to identify *coastal watersheds*. The methodology combined information on the extent of tidal influence (head of tide) and the U.S. Geological Survey's mapping of watersheds, identifying those 8-digit hydrologic unit watersheds that contained tidal water bodies. A similar method was used for Great Lakes wetlands using direct drainage to the Great Lakes instead of tidal effects. Because of the varying and complex state and federal laws governing the placement of coastal boundaries, closure of the hydrologic units was not provided by the Hydrologic Unit Maps along the coastline of the United States (Seaber et al. 1994). In this study, the outer coastal boundary was determined by the extent of the coastal sampling frame used by the FWS' National Wetlands Status and Trends Study for the Atlantic, Gulf of Mexico, and Great Lakes coastal areas. The inland study boundary coincided with the corresponding coastal watershed. The total area sampled in these three areas was 212.6 million acres[3] (Table 2).

TABLE 2. Area (in acres) of Coastal Watersheds in this Study.	
Coastal Watershed	**Area (acres)**
Atlantic	89,061,946
Gulf of Mexico	67,556,077
Great Lakes	55,936,677
Total Study Area	212,554,700

Wetland changes were determined by intensive analysis of the aerial imagery, interpretation of wetland types and hydrologic conditions, and determination of the changes that occurred between the respective target dates. The mean dates of the aerial imagery used to determine wetland trends were 1998 and 2004, with the difference being an average of 6 years. For this study, wetlands 1.0 acres and larger composed the target population.[4] Actual results indicated that for each wetland category included in the study, the minimum size represented was less than 1.0 acre. Additional information on the study design, data collection, and analysis procedures has been discussed by Dahl (2006).

Changes were recorded in areal extent or type of wetland observed on the sample plots between 1998 and 2004. Field verification of features on the aerial imagery was done for 824 plots (36 percent) during 2004 and 2005. Field verification addressed questions regarding image interpretation, land use coding, and attribution of wetland gains or losses. Field work was also performed as a quality control measure to verify that plot delineations were correct. Verification involved field visits to a variety of wetland types and geographical settings.

To reflect reliability, each estimate is accompanied by a percent coefficient variation expressed as a percent (i.e., there is a 95 percent probability that an estimate was within the indicated percentage range of the true value). The wetland area estimates generated for this study include all wetlands regardless of land ownership. ■

---

[3] This study incorporated some estuarine embayments not included in the total land area figure.
[4] Smaller wetlands were detected and included in the study, but it cannot be determined that all wetlands less than 1.0 acre were detected.

DEFINITIONS OF HABITAT CATEGORIES WITHIN COASTAL WATERSHEDS

WETLANDS

This study used the Fish and Wildlife Service definition of wetland (Cowardin *et al.* 1979). This definition is the national standard for wetland mapping, monitoring and data reporting as determined by the Federal Geographic Data Committee (2005). It is a two-part definition as indicated below:

Wetlands are lands transitional between terrestrial and aquatic systems where the water table is usually at or near the surface or the land is covered by shallow water.

For purposes of this classification wetlands must have one or more of the following three attributes: (1) at least periodically, the land supports predominantly hydrophytes, (2) the substrate is predominantly undrained hydric soil, and (3) the substrate is nonsoil and is saturated with water or covered by shallow water at some time during the growing season of each year.

Habitat category definitions are given in synoptic form in Table 3. The reader is encouraged to also review the Appendix, which provides complete definitions of wetland types and land use categories used in this study.

DEEPWATER HABITATS

Cowardin *et al.* (1979) consider wetlands and deepwater habitats separately; that is, the term wetland does not include deep, permanent water bodies. Deepwater habitats are permanently flooded land lying below the deepwater boundary of wetlands. Deepwater habitats include environments where surface water is permanent and often deep, so that water, rather than air, is the principal medium in which the dominant organisms live, whether or not they are attached to the substrate. In lacustrine and riverine systems, the boundary between deepwater and wetland habitats is approximately 2m (6.6 ft) below low water, or at the deepest extent of emergents, shrubs, or trees. For the purposes of this study, all lacustrine (lake) and riverine (river) waters without visible vegetation were considered deepwater habitats.

UPLAND HABITATS

An abbreviated upland classification system patterned after the U. S. Geological Survey land classification scheme described by Anderson *et al.* (1976), with five generalized categories, was used to describe uplands in this study. These categories are also listed in Table 3.

STUDY LIMITATIONS

Due to the limitations of using aerial imagery as the primary data source to detect wetlands, certain habitats were excluded from this study by design. These included:

REEFS — Tropical reef communities (coral or tuberficid worm reefs) occurred offshore in south Florida waters. These reefs ranged in water depth from less than 1 m to 41 m. Coral reefs were concentrated complexes of corals and other organisms that constructed a limestone structure in shallow waters (Jaap 1984). Reefs provided important links to fishery and benthic

TABLE 3. Wetland, deepwater, and upland categories used in this study. The definitions for each category appear in the Appendix.	
Salt Water Habitats	**Common Description**
Marine Subtidal*	Open Ocean
Marine Intertidal	Near shore
Estuarine Subtidal*	Open-water/bay bottoms
Estuarine Intertidal Emergents	Salt marsh
Estuarine Intertidal Forested/Shrub	Mangroves or other estuarine shrubs
Estuarine Intertidal Unconsolidated Shore	Beaches/bars/shoals
Riverine* (may be tidal or non-tidal)	River systems/channels
Freshwater Habitats	
Palustrine Forested	Forested wetlands
Palustrine Shrub	Shrub wetlands
Palustrine Emergents	Inland marshes/emergent wetlands
Palustrine Unconsolidated Shore	Shorelines/beaches/bars
Palustrine Unconsolidated Bottom	Open-water ponds
Palustrine farmed	Farmed wetland
Lacustrine*	Deepwater lakes and reservoirs
Uplands	
Agriculture	Cropland, pasture, managed rangeland
Urban	Cities and incorporated developments
Forested Plantations	Planted or intensively managed forests; silviculture
Rural Development	Non-urban developed areas and Infrastructure
Other Uplands	Rural uplands not in any other category; barren lands

*Constitutes deepwater habitat

marine resources and along with seagrasses and mangroves formed vital components of the coastal ecosystem (Miller and Crosby 1998). The only emergent coral reefs found in the conterminous U.S. were located in the Florida Keys extending south from Miami and Soldier Key to the Dry Tortugas. Coral reef extent and changes were not quantified as part of this study. Although data from other studies were available for only limited geographical sites, there has been widespread agreement that coral reef area has been declining (Millhouser et al. 1998).

Oyster (*Crassostrea virginica*) reefs also occurred in the intertidal zone adjacent to marshes or mud flats of mid and south Atlantic states and along the Gulf coast. There were also a number of artificially created reefs in coastal waters. The area of oyster reefs and artificial reefs were also not quantified in this study.

SEAGRASSES OR SUBMERGED AQUATIC VEGETATION — Detection of submerged aquatic vegetation required specialized techniques such as those described by Dierssen et al. (2003) to accurately determine the extent of seagrasses. Seagrasses and other submerged plants inhabited the intertidal and subtidal zones of estuaries and near shore coastal waters (Orth et al. 1990). Seagrasses have been used to characterize water quality because of their widespread distribution, important ecological niche and their sensitivity to water quality changes. The data presented in this report do not include area estimates of seagrasses or submerged aquatic vegetation.

EPHEMERAL WATER — Cowardin et al. (1979) did not recognize ephemeral water areas as a wetland type and ephemeral waters were not included in this study. This is consistent with other national Wetlands Status and Trends studies conducted by the Fish and Wildlife Service (Dahl 2006). ■

RESULTS: STATUS OF WETLANDS IN COASTAL WATERSHEDS

This study found that there were an estimated 39.8 million acres of wetlands in the coastal watersheds of the eastern United States in 2004. This represented 38 percent of the estimated total wetland acreage in the conterminous United States (Figure 2). Of all wetlands found in the coastal watersheds, 34.0 million acres (86 percent) were freshwater and 5.8 million acres (14 percent) were saltwater (estuarine or marine) as shown in Figure 3.

In the saltwater systems, estuarine emergents were the most prevalent type, making up an estimated 71 percent (4.1 million acres) of all estuarine and marine wetlands. Estuarine shrub wetlands comprised 14 percent of the area and non-vegetated saltwater wetlands 15 percent.

In the freshwater system, forested wetlands made up 62 percent of the total freshwater wetland area in the coastal watersheds. This was the single largest freshwater category by area. Other freshwater wetland types consisted of shrub wetlands that represented an estimated 19 percent of the total freshwater wetland area, emergents at 16 percent, and freshwater ponds at 3 percent.

FIGURE 2. Wetland Area of the Coastal Watersheds (Great Lakes, Atlantic and Gulf of Mexico) as a Percent of Total Wetland Area in the Conterminous United States, 2004.

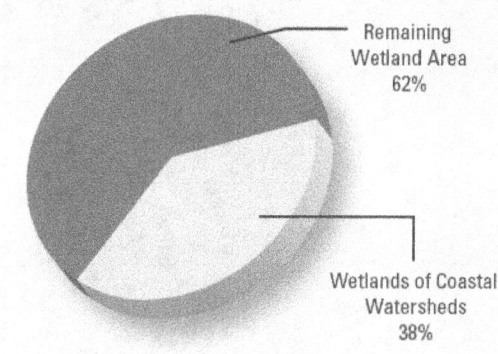

Remaining Wetland Area 62%

Wetlands of Coastal Watersheds 38%

FIGURE 3. Wetland Types in the Coastal Watersheds (Great Lakes, Atlantic and Gulf of Mexico), 2004.

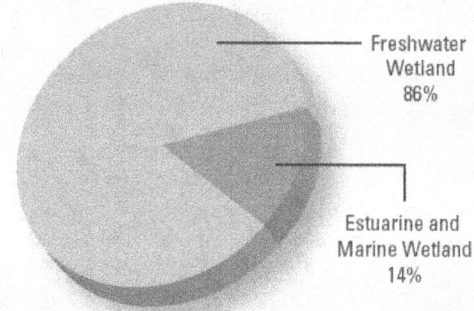

Freshwater Wetland 86%

Estuarine and Marine Wetland 14%

Watersheds of the Atlantic and Gulf of Mexico coasts have almost the same amount of total wetland area: 15.9 million and 15.6 million acres, respectively. Watersheds of the Great Lakes had an estimated 8.4 million acres. Not surprisingly, wetlands occupy more land area in some watersheds than in others (Figure 4).

Figure 4. Wetland density in the coastal watersheds of the Atlantic, Gulf of Mexico, and Great Lakes, 2004.

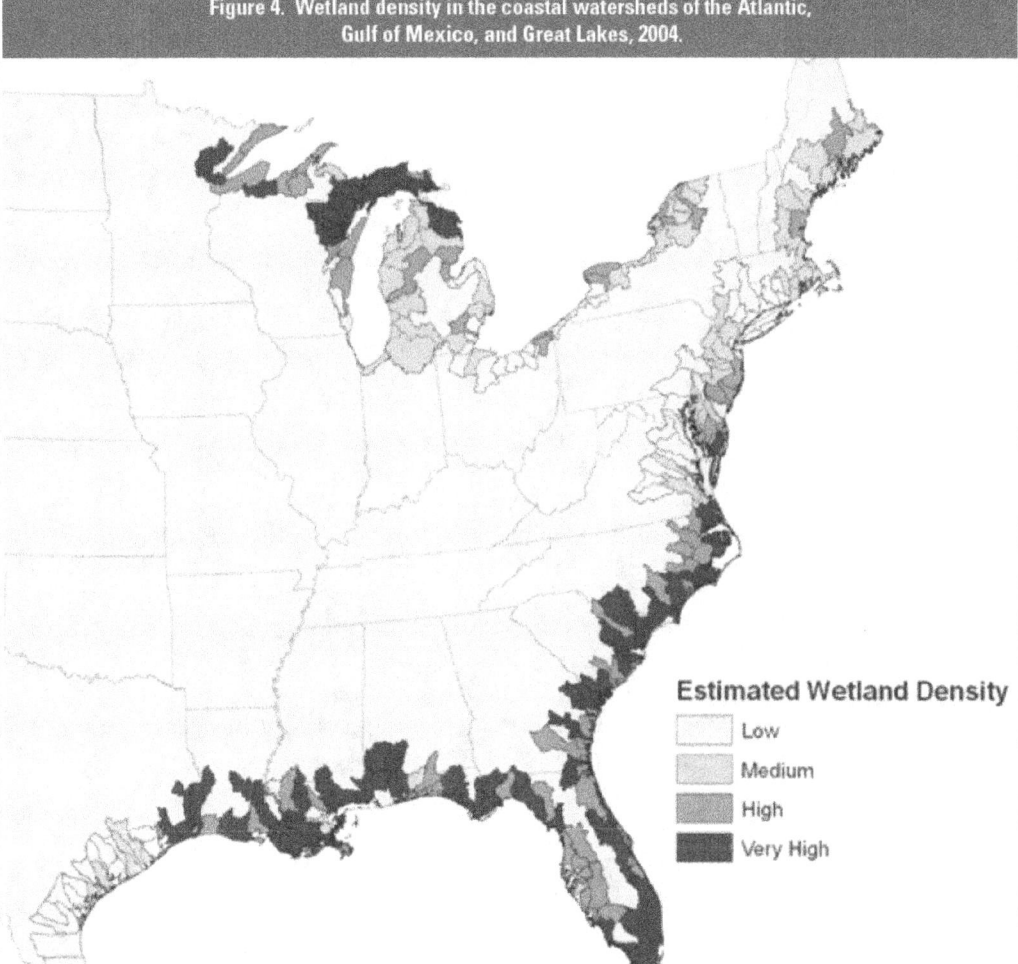

Estimated Wetland Density
- Low
- Medium
- High
- Very High

Low: <10%, Medium: 10.1–17.6%, High: 17.7–32.5%, and Very High: >32.6%.

The estimated changes in wetland area for the coastal watersheds of the Great Lakes, Atlantic, and Gulf of Mexico from 1998 to 2004 are shown in Table 4.

TABLE 4. Estimated change in wetland area for selected wetland categories for Coastal Watersheds of the Great Lakes, Atlantic, and Gulf of Mexico, 1998 to 2004. The coefficient of variation (CV) for each entry (expressed as a percentage) is given in parentheses.				
	Area in Acres			
Wetland Category	**Estimated Area, 1998**	**Estimated Area, 2004**	**Change, 1998 to 2004**	**Change (percent)**
Marine Intertidal	135,970 (18.8)	134,180 (19.0)	-1,860 (69.9)	-1.4
Estuarine Intertidal Non-vegetated[1]	699,390 (12.3)	704,660 (11.9)	+5,270 (*)	+0.7
Estuarine Intertidal Vegetated[2]	4,950,430	4,885,450	-64,970	-1.3
All Intertidal (Saltwater) Wetlands	5,818,260	5,756,700	-61,560	-1.1
Freshwater Non-vegetated[3]	960,980	1,139,940	+178,960	+1.6
Freshwater Forested	21,064,220 (3.7)	21,100,450 (3.7)	+36,230 (*)	+0.2
Freshwater Shrub	6,735,910 (5.4)	6,293,530 (5.7)	-422,380 (42.5)	-6.6
Freshwater Emergent	5,612,020 (7.0)	5,539,680 (7.0)	-72,340 (101.3)	-1.3
Freshwater Vegetated Wetlands[4]	33,412,150	32,933,650	-478,500	-1.4
All Freshwater Wetlands	34,373,130	34,073,600	-299,540	-0.9
All Wetlands	40,191,380	39,830,280	-361,100	-0.9

*Statistically unreliable

[1] Includes the category: Estuarine Intertidal Unconsolidated Shore.

[2] Includes the categories: Estuarine Intertidal Emergent and Estuarine Intertidal Shrub.

[3] Includes the categories: Palustrine Aquatic Bed, Palustrine Unconsolidated Bottom and Palustrine Unconsolidated Shore.

[4] Includes the categories: Palustrine Emergent, Palustrine Forested and Palustrine Shrub.

Considering saltwater and freshwater systems together, there was an estimated loss of 361,100 wetland acres in the coastal watersheds between 1998 and 2004. Both the Atlantic and the Gulf of Mexico coasts experienced net wetland losses of 14,980 and 370,760 acres, respectively. The Great Lakes coastal watersheds had an estimated net gain of 24,650 acres. For all three coastal watersheds, this equated to an average annual net loss of about 60,000 acres over the 6-year period of this study. There were wetlands gains in each of the coastal regions, but wetland losses far outweighed the gains, especially in the Gulf of Mexico (Figure 5).

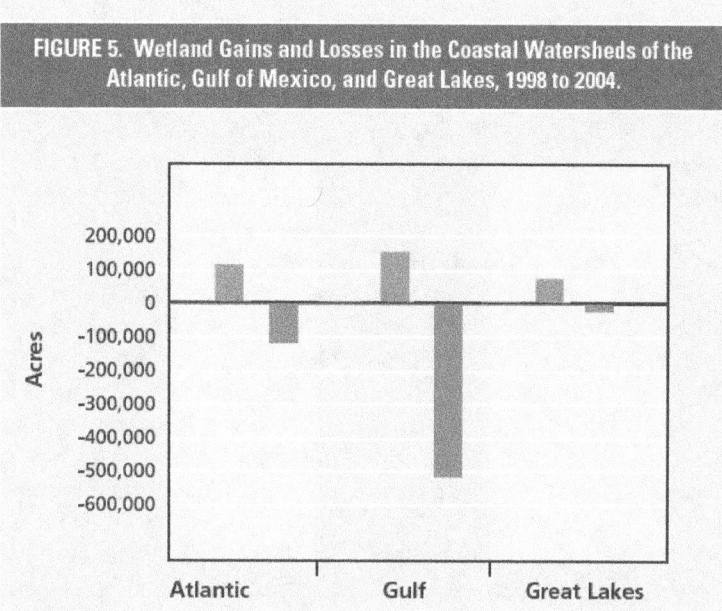

FIGURE 5. Wetland Gains and Losses in the Coastal Watersheds of the Atlantic, Gulf of Mexico, and Great Lakes, 1998 to 2004.

TRENDS IN COASTAL SALTWATER WETLANDS – 1998 TO 2004

Because Cowardin *et al.* (1979) defines "estuarine" and "marine" wetlands as saltwater systems, no estuarine or marine wetlands were identified in the coastal watersheds of the Great Lakes portion of this study. Shoreline wetlands of the Great Lakes were included with other freshwater wetlands in the Great Lakes coastal watersheds.

The majority of estuarine and marine wetlands fall into three types: estuarine intertidal emergent wetlands (salt and brackish water marshes), estuarine shrub wetlands (mangrove swamps and other salt-tolerant woody species), and estuarine and marine intertidal non-vegetated wetlands. The latter category included exposed coastal beaches subject to tidal flooding, as well as sand bars, tidal mud flats, shoals, and sand spits.

Coastal wetlands are subjected to a multitude of anthropogenic stressors originating from the landward side, as well as natural forces affecting change from the sea. Stressors originating from land-based activities include dredging, filling, shoreline hardening, and a multitude of other human activities that destroy wetlands. Seaward, events such as coastal storms, tidal surge causing erosion and deposition, saltwater intrusion, and inundation have the ability to modify coastal wetland type and extent. Kennish (2004) has summarized the major threats to estuarine environments that include habitat loss, introduction of contaminants, invasive species, freshwater diversion, sea level rise, and subsidence, among others. EPA also has provided indicators of coastal condition and identified sources of environmental degradation affecting coastal ecosystems to include discharges from municipalities and industries and nonpoint-source runoff (EPA 2008).

Between 1998 and 2004, saltwater wetlands declined by slightly more than 1.0 percent. Estimated estuarine and marine wetland losses (all intertidal wetland types) were over twice as great along the Gulf of Mexico as compared to the Atlantic coast (Table 5). Over 44,000 acres of these saltwater wetlands were lost in Gulf of Mexico coastal watersheds during this study period.

The results from this study indicated that intertidal marine non-vegetated wetland area (tidal flats and shoals) declined by an estimated 6.0 percent along the coastal areas of the Gulf of Mexico, whereas they remained stable along the coastal areas of the Atlantic.

The Gulf of Mexico had an estimated 36 percent more area of saltwater wetland than the Atlantic in 2004. The watersheds along the Gulf of Mexico contained greater area of all wetland types with the exception of marine intertidal flats and shoals. Both the Atlantic and Gulf of Mexico coasts lost saltwater vegetated wetlands between 1998 and 2004. Estuarine intertidal vegetated wetland (saltwater marsh and shrubs) in both of these regions declined by an estimated 65,000 acres (1.3 percent) overall.

Estuarine emergents (salt marsh) sustained the largest losses, declining by an estimated 1.0 and 1.8 percent in the Atlantic and Gulf of Mexico, respectively. Estuarine salt marsh exhibited the largest declines of any saltwater wetland type on both the Atlantic and Gulf of Mexico coasts, declining by an estimated 62,500 acres. The ecological value of estuarine salt marsh wetlands has been well documented by a number of researchers (Livingston 1984; Montague and Wiegert 1990; Watzin and Gosselink 1992; Mitsch and Gosselink 2000; EPA 2008). The total monetary value of coastal wetlands for storm protection has been evaluated by Costanza *et al.* (2008). These studies indicate that the loss of coastal wetland area has had adverse ecological and economic effects.

TABLE 5. Estimated Changes to Saltwater (Estuarine and Marine) Wetlands in the Coastal Watersheds of the Atlantic and Gulf of Mexico Coasts, 1998 to 2004. Percent Coefficient of Variation was Expressed as (Standard Deviation/Mean) X 100.

Estimated Changes to Saltwater Wetlands of the Atlantic Coast				
	Area in Acres			
Atlantic Coast—Wetland Category	Estimated Area, 1998	Estimated Area, 2004	Change, 1998 to 2004	Change (percent)
Marine Intertidal	105,130 (21.9)	105,160 (21.9)	+30 (71.4)	–
Estuarine Non-vegetated[1]	287,920 (21.4)	287,680 (20.8)	-240 (*)	-0.1
Estuarine Emergent	1,722,900 (6.0)	1,704,460 (6.0)	-18,430 (*)	-1.0
Estuarine Shrub	119,430 (16.6)	118,320 (16.6)	-1,110 (*)	-0.9
Estuarine Vegetated[2]	1,842.320 (5.8)	1,822,780 (5.7)	-19,540 (*)	-1.0
All Intertidal Wetlands – Atlantic	2,267,850 (6.1)	2,248,100 (6.0)	-19,750 (*)	-0.9

Estimated Changes to Saltwater Wetlands of the Gulf of Mexico Coast				
	Area in Acres			
Wetland Category	Estimated Area, 1998	Estimated Area, 2004	Change, 1998 to 2004	Change (percent)
Marine Intertidal	30,830 (38.2)	28,950 (40.3)	-1,890 (68.8)	-6.1
Estuarine Non-vegetated[1]	411,470 (14.5)	416,980 (14.1)	+5,510 (*)	+1.3
Estuarine Emergent	2,428,970 (5.8)	2,384,880 (5.9)	-44,090 (20.0)	-1.8
Estuarine Shrub	679,140 (14.8)	677,800 (14.8)	-1,340 (69.6)	-0.2
Estuarine Vegetated[2]	3,108,110 (5.6)	3,062,680 (5.7)	-45,430 (19.4)	-1.5
All Intertidal Wetlands – Gulf of Mexico Coast	3,550,400 (5.2)	3,508,600 (5.3)	-44,810 (24.7)	-1.2

*Statistically unreliable
[1] Includes Estuarine Intertidal Unconsolidated Shore
[2] Sum of Estuarine Emergent and Estuarine Shrub

Most saltwater wetland losses from both the Atlantic and the Gulf of Mexico resulted from inundation or saltwater intrusion (Figure 5). This was observed most extensively in a region of the Atlantic coast extending south from Rhode Island Sound to the mouth of Chesapeake Bay, which included areas along the coastal states of New York, New Jersey, Delaware, Maryland, and Virginia. Wetlands were also lost to open saltwater in the western Gulf of Mexico, principally along the coastlines of Mississippi, Louisiana, and Texas. These findings coincide with the Coastal Vulnerability Index for the U.S. Atlantic coast that shows the relative vulnerability of the coast to changes due to future rise in sea level (Thieler and Hammar-Klose 1999).

Along the coastal fringe there are regional differences in geomorphology, land use, and development trends. This may explain why certain regions of the Atlantic coastline seemed to be particularly susceptible to wetland loss as a result of inundation or saltwater intrusion. Thieler and Hammar-Klose (1999) found portions of the Chesapeake Bay region vulnerable to sea-level rise as a result of low coastal slope, saltwater wetland as a common landform type, and a relatively high rate of sea-level rise. In contrast, the coastline of New England may be much less vulnerable to sea-level rise due to its steep coastal slope, rocky shoreline, and larger tidal range.

It has been speculated that the process of coastal wetland retreat caused by saltwater inundation may be more prevalent along the southeastern coastal plain than in the northern Atlantic region. Williams et al. (1999) found that along portions of the west coast of Florida, saltwater intrusion might be replacing forested habitats with salt marsh or more salt tolerant species—perhaps a more subtle ecological shift than the drowning of coastal vegetation by rising sea levels associated with saltwater inundation. However, the results from this study did not find coastal saltwater wetland losses due to inundation or saltwater intrusion along the coastal plain of the southeastern Atlantic, nor on the Florida coastline of the Gulf of Mexico. Intertidal wetlands lost to open saltwater were most prevalent in the northern to mid-Atlantic regions, for reasons undetermined by this study.

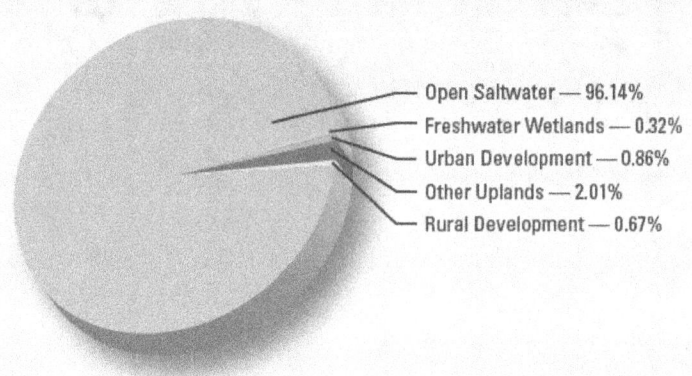

FIGURE 6. Attribution of loss or conversion of saltwater wetlands in the coastal watersheds of the Atlantic and Gulf of Mexico, 1998 to 2004.

Open Saltwater — 96.14%
Freshwater Wetlands — 0.32%
Urban Development — 0.86%
Other Uplands — 2.01%
Rural Development — 0.67%

There were small losses of saltwater wetlands attributable to development or other direct human activities. Estimated losses of these types to urban and rural development was 1.5 percent of all saltwater wetland losses recorded during the period of this study. Many federal and state agencies are involved in the regulation, protection, and monitoring of saltwater wetlands, coastal areas, and the species that inhabit them. Additionally, coastal states also have established coastal zone management plans, growth management plans, and coastal resource agencies (Dahl 2000). These programs and policies appear to have been effective in limiting development in saltwater wetlands. There was also very little wetland area restored in the intertidal systems of the Atlantic or Gulf of Mexico between 1998 and 2004. The most notable gains in saltwater wetlands were the result of conversion from deepwater and freshwater wetlands along the Atlantic coast, although these gains in area were negated by losses to open saltwater on both coastlines. Wetland restoration (re-establishment) or creation is more problematic in the coastal watersheds, where land values fueled by continued development are high. Additionally, successful restoration of many coastal wetlands hinges on consideration of physical processes including flow, circulation, transport of nutrients, salinity, and sediments (Sanders and Arega 2002).

Trends in Freshwater Coastal Wetlands – 1998 to 2004

An estimated 33 percent of all freshwater wetland area in the conterminous United States is found in the coastal watersheds of the eastern United States (Table 6). Freshwater emergent wetlands generally contained shallow water and were dominated by herbaceous plants. They included areas known as marsh, swale, slough, wet prairie, wet savanna, reed swamps, and glades. Freshwater emergent wetland area declined in all coastal watersheds between 1998 and 2004.

	Wetland Area in Acres		
Wetland Category	Coastal Watersheds 2004	Conterminous U.S. 2004	% Wetland Area in Coastal Watersheds, 2004
Freshwater Non-Vegetated[1]	1,139,940	6,229,600	18%
Freshwater Forested	21,100,450	52,031,400	41%
Freshwater Shrub	6,293,530	17,641,400	36%
Freshwater Emergent	5,539,680	26,147,000	21%
Freshwater Vegetated Wetland[2]	32,933,650	95,819,800	34%
All Freshwater Wetlands	34,073,580	102,453,800	33%

TABLE 6. Estimated Freshwater Wetland Acreage for Coastal Watersheds of the Atlantic, Gulf of Mexico and Great Lakes as Compared to the Conterminous United States, 2004.

[1] Includes the categories: Palustrine Aquatic Bed, Palustrine Unconsolidated Bottom and Palustrine Unconsolidated Shore.

[2] Includes the categories: Palustrine Emergent, Palustrine Forested and Palustrine Shrub.

Freshwater wetlands in coastal watersheds exhibited trends similar to those occurring elsewhere in the nation. Non-vegetated freshwater ponds, both natural and artificial, increased in area. Estimated pond acreage increased by 18.0, 19.4, and 19.3 percent in the Atlantic, Gulf of Mexico, and Great Lakes coastal watersheds, respectively (Table 7).

Collectively, freshwater wetlands in coastal watersheds declined by an estimated 0.9 percent between 1998 and 2004. Freshwater shrubs declined the most of any freshwater wetland type, as an estimated 442,400 acres were lost during the period of this study. Large losses of this freshwater wetland type in the Atlantic and Gulf of Mexico coastal watersheds accounted for this decline. There was a net gain in wetland shrub area in the Great Lakes. The freshwater vegetated wetlands (forest, shrub, and emergent types) found in all watersheds included in this study declined by an estimated 1.4 percent, whereas freshwater ponds increased by almost 1.6 percent.

TABLE 7. Estimated Changes to Freshwater Wetlands in the Coastal Watersheds of the Atlantic, Gulf of Mexico and Great Lakes, 1998 to 2004. Percent Coefficient of Variation was Expressed as (Standard Deviation/Mean) X 100

Estimated Changes to Freshwater Wetlands in Coastal Watersheds of the Atlantic Coast, 1998 to 2004

Wetland Category	Area in Acres			
	Estimated Area, 1998	Estimated Area, 2004	Change, 1998 to 2004	Change (percent)
Freshwater Non-vegetated (ponds)[1]	404,300 (7.6)	475,370 (9.2)	+71,070 (31.2)	+18.0
Freshwater Forested	8,454,700 (4.9)	8,771,720 (4.8)	+317,020 (85.4)	+3.7
Freshwater Shrub	3,000,320 (7.9)	2,627,630 (8.2)	-372,690 (33.0)	-12.0
Freshwater Emergent	1,799,940 (10.9)	1,789,300 (10.9)	-10,630 (*)	-0.6
Freshwater Vegetated[2]	13,254,960 (4.0)	13,188,660 (4.0)	-66,300 (*)	-0.5
All Freshwater Wetlands	13,659,260 (3.9)	13,664,030 (3.8)	+4,770 (*)	+0.03
All Wetlands (Atlantic Coast Watersheds)[3]	15,927,100 (3.4)	15,912,120 3.4	-14,980 (*)	-0.1

Estimated Changes to Wetlands in Coastal Watersheds of the Gulf of Mexico Coast, 1998 to 2004

Wetland Category	Area in Acres			
	Estimated Area, 1998	Estimated Area, 2004	Change, 1998 to 2004	Change (percent)
Freshwater Non-vegetated (ponds)[1]	349,210 (6.9)	417,030 (7.5)	+67,820 (18.1)	+19.4
Freshwater Forested	7,453,120 (4.8)	7,324,780 (5.1)	-128,340 (77.5)	-1.7
Freshwater Shrub	1,800,690 (8.6)	1,581,930 (8.9)	-218,760 (28.0)	-12.2
Freshwater Emergent	2,779,720 (9.9)	2,730,050 (9.9)	-49,670 (67.3)	-1.8
Freshwater Vegetated[2]	12,033,530 (4.1)	11,636,760 (4.2)	-396,770 (24.0)	-3.3
All Freshwater Wetlands	12,382,740 (4.0)	12,053,790 (4.0)	-328,950 (28.9)	-2.7
All Wetlands (Gulf of Mexico Coast Watersheds)[3]	15,933,140 (3.3)	15,562,400 (3.3)	-370,760 (25.8)	-2.3

TABLE 7. Estimated Changes to Freshwater Wetlands in the Coastal Watersheds of the Atlantic, Gulf of Mexico and Great Lakes, 1998 to 2004. Percent Coefficient of Variation was Expressed as (Standard Deviation/Mean) X 100 *(continued)*

Estimated Changes to Wetland Area for Freshwater Wetlands in Coastal Watersheds of the Great Lakes, 1998 to 2004

Wetland Category	Area in Acres			
	Estimated Area, 1998	Estimated Area, 2004	Change, 1998 to 2004	Change (percent)
Freshwater Non-vegetated (ponds)[1]	207,470 (12.1)	247,540 (10.0)	+40,570 (22.7)	+19.3
Freshwater Forested	5,156,400 (9.8)	5,003,950 (9.8)	-152,450 (75.0)	-3.0
Freshwater Shrub	1,934,900 (12.0)	2,083,970 (12.4)	+149,060 (76.2)	+7.7
Freshwater Emergent	1,032,360 (12.4)	1,020,320 (12.6)	-12,040 (*)	-1.0
Freshwater Vegetated[2]	8,123,660 (8.2)	8,108,240 (8.2)	-15,430 (74.6)	-0.2
All Freshwater Wetlands (Great Lakes Watersheds)	8,331,130 (8.0)	8,355,780 (7.9)	+24,650 (44.0)	+0.3

*Estimate statistically unreliable.

[1] Includes the categories: Palustrine Aquatic Bed, Palustrine Unconsolidated Bottom, and Palustrine Unconsolidated Shore

[2] Includes the categories: Palustrine Forested, Palustrine Shrub and Palustrine Emergent

[3] Includes all freshwater and saltwater wetlands

In the Great Lakes and the Atlantic regions, freshwater forested and shrub wetlands reflect acreage changes (interchange between wetland shrub and forested categories) largely as a result of areas being harvested for timber and becoming shrub wetlands, then maturing and returning as forested wetlands. Forest and shrub wetland area gains and losses were almost equal between 1998 and 2004 in the Great Lakes and Atlantic. Forested wetlands of the Gulf of Mexico region were represented by many different ecological associations, and included wet pine flatwoods, mixed hardwoods, river swamps, cypress domes, and hydric hammocks. These forested resources sustained substantial losses overall.

Overall, the Gulf of Mexico coastal watersheds exhibited substantial losses in freshwater wetlands. An estimated 396,800 acres of freshwater vegetated wetlands were lost between 1998 and 2004. This rate of loss was 6 times higher than the rate of freshwater vegetated wetlands losses in the Atlantic coastal watersheds. The estimated wetland losses for all wetland types in the Gulf of Mexico were almost 25 times higher than those estimates for the Atlantic (371,000 acres versus 15,000 acres lost) over the course of this study (Figure 7 on page 24).

The losses of all freshwater wetlands for the Atlantic, Gulf of Mexico, and Great Lakes coastal watersheds have been attributed to various causes, as shown in Figure 8. Coastal development in both rural and urban areas, loss to deepwater habitats (reservoirs), silvicultural activities, drainage, and filling for other types of development contributed to the losses of

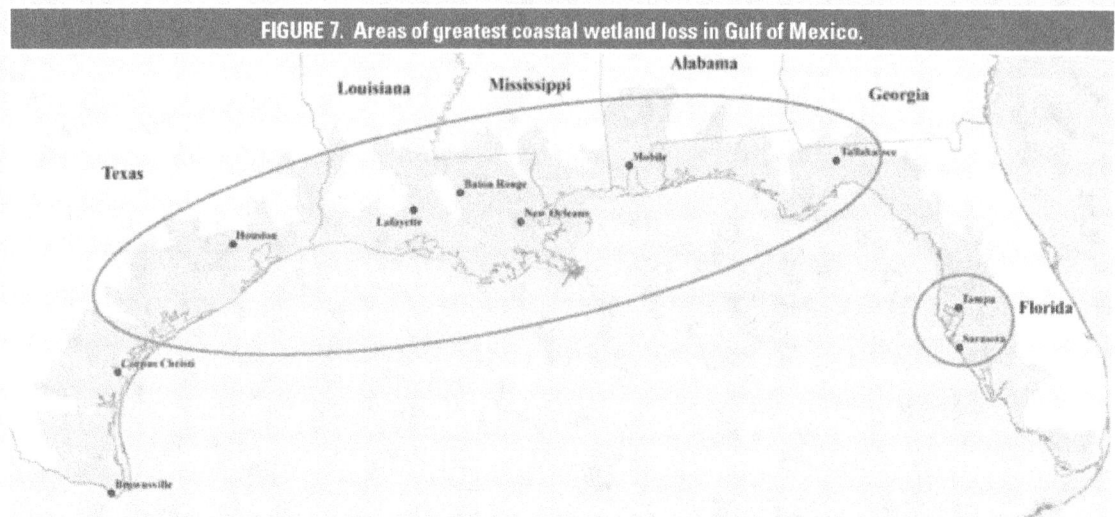

FIGURE 7. Areas of greatest coastal wetland loss in Gulf of Mexico.

coastal freshwater wetlands along the Gulf of Mexico. The population of coastal counties in the Gulf Coast region increased more than 100 percent between 1960 and 2000 (U.S. Census Bureau 2003). Because a disproportionate percentage of the nation's population lives in coastal areas, activities that support municipalities, commerce, industry, and tourism have created environmental pressures (EPA 2005). These development pressures have resulted in substantial physical changes along many areas of the coast, and coastal wetlands continue to be lost to residential and commercial development (EPA 2008).

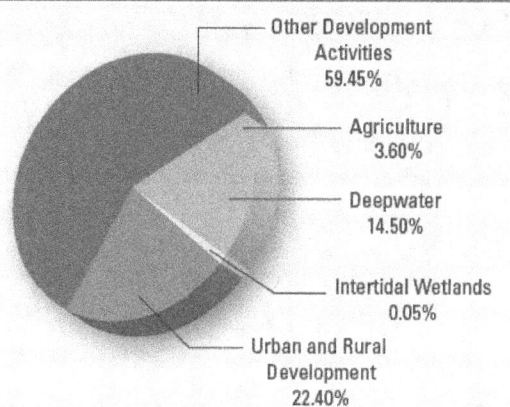

FIGURE 8. Attribution of Loss or Conversion of Freshwater Wetlands in the Coastal Watersheds of the Atlantic, Gulf of Mexico and Great Lakes, 1998 to 2004

- Other Development Activities 59.45%
- Agriculture 3.60%
- Deepwater 14.50%
- Intertidal Wetlands 0.05%
- Urban and Rural Development 22.40%

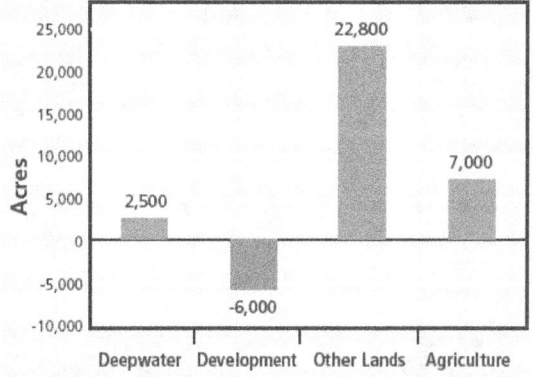

FIGURE 9. Net Gains and Losses (in acres) of Coastal Wetlands in the Great Lakes Coastal Watersheds, 1998 to 2004.

Estimated net gains in freshwater wetland area were seen in both the Great Lakes and the Atlantic coastal watersheds. The Atlantic coastal region gained about 4,800 acres of freshwater wetlands between 1998 and 2004. The Great Lakes had the largest estimated increase in freshwater wetland area. There was a net gain of an estimated 24,650 acres over the study period, with wetland area coming from fresh deepwater habitats, agricultural lands, and the other uplands category (Figure 9).

CASE STUDY: RESTORATION OF FLORIDA'S ST. VINCENT ISLAND

In 2008, NOAA, FWS, the Fish America Foundation, and other partners restored a large area of St. Vincent Island, a 12,000 acre barrier island in the Gulf of Mexico. Nearly 2,000 acres of wetland needed to be restored as a result of 45 miles of roads blocking natural tidal flow for many years. These wetlands and the surrounding Apalachicola Bay serve as a nursery for a wide variety of fish species, including the striped bass, Gulf sturgeon, tarpon, red drum, spotted seatrout and Gulf flounder. St. Vincent Island also provides sanctuary for a number of endangered and threatened species. Loggerhead, green, and leatherback sea turtles come ashore to nest on its beaches, and wood storks stop here during their migrations.

Restoration on an island is extremely complicated logistically. All machinery, equipment, and personnel had to be barged to the island, offloaded at the docking location, and then hauled to the far end of the island where the work took place. Working in marine conditions created additional challenges, as the harsh saline environment increased wear and equipment break-downs, the soft sediment made it difficult to move machinery, and the sensitivity of the surrounding environment required special consideration be given to methods and best management practices. All of these factors added to the cost and time required to complete the restoration.

Today, swaths of wetlands are recovering natural function across areas once blocked by roads and disrupted by water diversion. Birds and fish are also returning as tidal flow returns to normal and water quality improves. In combination with neighboring restoration efforts at Tates Hell State Forest, St. Joe Bay Buffer Preserve and Florida Fish and Wildlife Commission's Apalachicola Wildlife and Environmental Area, the St. Vincent Island restoration will ensure that the entire region benefits from this conservation success. ▪

Figure 10. St. Vincent Island restoration site, Florida, post-restoration.

SUMMARY AND CONCLUSIONS

Coastal watersheds of the eastern United States contained about 11 percent of the total land area in the lower 48 states and 38 percent of the wetlands by area. Yet these coastal areas experienced roughly the same amount of wetland loss from 1998 to 2004 as occurred in the entire conterminous United States in the 1990s. As with other status and trends reports on wetland acreage trends, these data do not address the functionality of the wetlands lost, gained, or remaining unchanged in acreage.

More than half of the U.S. population lives in coastal areas, and people continue to move to coastal areas every year. Development was a major factor in the loss of coastal wetlands, especially along the Atlantic and Gulf of Mexico coasts, where it was the overwhelming factor in the loss of freshwater wetlands.

Rising sea level, coastal subsidence, and erosion processes were also important factors affecting wetland loss and distribution, especially along coastlines where the wetlands cannot migrate inland because the shorelines are artificially hardened or too steep. Coastal wetlands also appear to be vulnerable to saltwater inundation in areas of the northern to mid-Atlantic and the western Gulf of Mexico. To fully recognize the impacts of climate change on coastal wetlands, there will need to be a better understanding of the linkages among upland, wetland, and oceanic responses to changing conditions.

A majority of the coastal wetland loss (61,800 acres per year) from 1998 to 2004 occurred in the Gulf of Mexico. The loss of wetlands in southern Louisiana, estimated at about 18,500 acres per year (U.S. Geological Survey 1995) accounted for only about one-third of the wetland losses observed; much of the remaining losses occurred in the upper portions of the watersheds and were due to a combination of human-induced factors including urban and rural development, silvicultural operations, and other activities that drained or filled wetlands. In effect, the same human uses that are desired of coastal habitats are reducing their area and lessening their value.

That is not to say that wetland losses are not occurring in interior of the conterminous United States as well. But those losses have been offset by wetland gains that have resulted from re-establishment and creation in inland regions, whereas in the coastal watersheds of the Atlantic and Gulf of Mexico they have not been similarly offset. Wetland restoration in coastal areas is generally more expensive and logistically more difficult than wetland restoration in inland areas due, in part, to higher land costs, fewer suitable sites, and competing interests (e.g., development). Additionally, successful restoration of many coastal wetlands hinges on consideration of physical processes including flow, circulation, transport of nutrients, salinity, and sediments (Sanders and Arega 2002).

However, the results of this study suggest that wetland protection and restoration require more attention in coastal watersheds. Otherwise, there is a risk of reducing or losing the substantial ecological, commercial, economic, and recreational services they provide. Public policymakers and coastal managers have been confronted with the daily task of finding a balance between benefiting from economic growth and mitigating the effects of growth on coastal environments. This task will become more challenging as the coastal population continues to grow in a limited space, thereby exacting more pressure on the remaining natural habitats, including wetlands. ▪

REFERENCES CITED

Alexander, C.E., M.A. Broutman, and D.W. Field. 1986. An inventory of coastal wetlands of the USA. Rockville, MD: NOAA, National Ocean Service.

Anderson, J.R., E.E. Hardy, J.T. Roach, and R.E. Winter. 1976. A land use and land cover classification system for use with remote sensor data. U.S. Geological Survey Professional Paper 964. U.S. Geological Survey, Washington, D.C. 28 p.

Brady, S.J. and C.H. Flather. 1994. Changes in wetlands on nonfederal rural land of the conterminous United States from 1982 to 1987. Environmental Management, Vol. 18, No. 5, pp. 693-705.

Brady, S.J. and J.J. Goebel. 2002. Geographical distribution of wetland changes in the U.S., 1992-1997. 5th Wetlands Workshop, Atlantic City, NJ.

Costanza, R.,O. Perez-Maqueo, M.L. Martinez, P. Sutton, S.J. Anderson and K. Mulder. 2008. The value of coastal wetlands for hurricane protection. Ambio. Vol. 37, No. 4. pp. 241-248.

Council on Environmental Quality. 2008. Conserving America's Wetlands 2008. The White House Council on Environmental Quality. 57 p.

Cowardin, L.M, V. Carter, F.C. Golet, and E.T. LaRoe. 1979. Classification of wetlands and deepwater habitats of the United States. Department of the Interior, U.S. Fish and Wildlife Service, Washington, D.C. 131 p.

Crossett, K.M., T.J. Culliton, P.C. Wiley, and T.R. Goodspeed. 2004. Population Trends Along the Coastal United States: 1980-2008, Coastal Trends Report Series. NOAA, National Ocean Service, Silver Spring, MD. 51 p.

Dahl, T.E. 2000. Status and trends of wetlands in the conterminous United States 1986 to 1997. U.S. Department of the Interior, Fish and Wildlife Service, Washington, D.C. 82 pp.

Dahl, T.E. 2006. Status and trends of wetlands in the conterminous United States 1998 to 2004. U.S. Department of the Interior, Fish and Wildlife Service, Washington D.C. 112 p.

Dierssen, H. R., R.C. Zimmerman, R.A. Leathers, T.V. Downes, and C.O. Davis. 2003. Ocean color remote sensing of seagrass and bathymetry in the Bahamas Banks by high-resolution airborne imagery. Limnology and Oceanography, 48(1, part 2), pp. 444-455.

U. S. Environmental Protection Agency. 2005. National Coastal Condition Report II. Office of Research and Development/ Office of Water EPA-620/R-03/002. Washington, D.C. 286 p. http://www.epa.gov/owow/oceans/nccr2/

U. S. Environmental Protection Agency (EPA). 2008. National Coastal Condition Report III. Office of Research and Development/ Office of Water EPA/842-R-08-002. Washington, D.C. 295 p.

Federal Geographic Data Committee. 2005. (http://www.fgdc.gov/standards/projects/FGDC-standards-projects/wetlands/fgdc-announce).

Field, D.W., A.J. Reyer, P.V. Genovese, and B.D. Shearer. 1991. Coastal wetlands of the United States: an accounting of a valuable resource. NOAA, National Ocean Service, Silver Spring, MD. 59 p.

U.S. Fish and Wildlife Service (FWS). 1995. Coastal Ecosystems Program. Branch of Coastal and Wetland Resources, Division of Habitat Conservation, Washington, D.C. 48 p.

Gosselink, J.G. and R.H. Baumann. 1980. Wetland inventories: wetland loss along the United States coast. Z. Geomorph, N.F. pp. 173-187.

Jaap, W.C. 1984. The ecology of the south Florida coral reefs: A community profile. U.S. Fish and Wildlife Service, Washington, D.C. FWS/OBS 82/08. 138 p.

Kennish, M.J. 2004. Estuarine Research, Monitoring, and Resource Protection. CRC Press, Boca Raton, FL. 297 p.

Langbein, W.B. and K.T Iseri. 1960. General introduction and hydrologic definitions manual of hydrology. Part 1. General surface water techniques. U.S. Geological Survey, Water-Supply Paper 1541-A, Reston, VA. 29 p.

Lellis-Dibble, K.A., McGlynn, K.E., and Bigford, T.E. 2008. Estuarine Fish and Shellfish Species in U.S. Commercial and Recreational Fisheries: Economic Value as an Incentive to Protect and Restore Estuarine Habitat. In press.

Livingston, R. J. 1984. The ecology of the Apalachicola Bay system: An estuarine profile. U.S. Department of the Interior, Fish and Wildlife Service, FWS/OBS-82/05, Washington, D.C. 148 p.

Miller, S.L. and M.Y. Crosby. 1998. The extent and condition of U.S. coral reefs - NOAA's State of the Coast Report. NOAA, Silver Spring, MD.

Millhouser, W.C., J. McDonough, J.P. Tolson, and D. Slade. 1998. Managing coastal resources NOAA's State of the Coast Report. NOAA, Silver Spring, MD.

Mitsch, W.J. and J.G. Gosselink. 2000. Wetlands (3rd edition). John Wiley and Sons, Inc.

Montague, C.L. and R.G. Wiegert. 1990. Salt marshes. In Myers, R.L. and J.J. Ewel (Eds.) Ecosystems of Florida . University of Central Florida Press, Orlando, FL. pp. 481–516.

National Research Council. 1997. Striking a Balance: Improving Stewardship of Marine Areas. National Academy Press, Washington, DC.

National Oceanic and Atmospheric Administration (NOAA). 2005. Habitat Change Analysis. NOAA, National Ocean Service, Silver Spring, MD. 286 p.

NOAA. 2008. NOAA Coastal Change Analysis Program, Land Cover Analysis. http://www.csc.noaa.gov/crs/lca/ccap.html

Orth, R.J., K.A. Moore and J .E Nowak. 1990. Monitoring seagrass distribution and abundance patterns: A case study from the Chesapeake Bay. In S.J. Kiraly, EA. Cross and J.D. Buffington (Eds.). Federal coastal wetland mapping programs. Biol. Rept. 90 (18). Department of the Interior, U. S. Fish and Wildlife Service, Washington, D.C. pp. 111–123.

Pendleton, L. 2008. The Economic and Market Value of Coasts and Estuaries: What's at Stake? Restore America's Estuaries, Arlington, VA, 182 pp.

Reed, P.B. 1988. National list of plant species that occur in wetlands: 1988 National Summary. Biol. Rept. 88 (24). U.S. Fish and Wildlife Service, Washington, D.C. 244 p.

Sanders, B.F. and F. Arega. 2002. Hydrodynamic design in coastal wetland restoration. California Water Resources Center, University of CA, Irvine. Technical Completion Report - Project UCAL-WRC-W-942. 15 p.

Seaber, P.R., F.P. Kapinos, and G.L. Knapp. 1994. Hydrologic Unit Maps. U.S. Geological Survey Water- Supply Paper 2294. U.S. Department of the Interior, Geological Survey, Reston, VA. 63 p.

Shaw, S.P. and C.G. Fredine. 1956. Wetlands of the United States. U.S. Department of the Interior, Fish and Wildlife Service. Washington, D.C. Circular 39. 67 p.

Stedman, S.M., and J. Hanson. 2000. Habitat Connections: Wetlands, fisheries and economics in the South Atlantic Coastal States. National Oceanic and Atmospheric Administration, National Marine Fisheries Service. http://www.nmfs.noaa.gov/habitat/habitatconservation/publications/habitatconections/num2.htm.

Thieler, E. R. and E. S. Hammar-Klose. 1999. National Assessment of Coastal Vulnerability to Sea-Level Rise: Preliminary Results for the U.S. Atlantic Coast. U.S. Geological Survey Open-File Report 99-593, Woods Hole, MA. http://pubs.usgs.gov/of/1999/of99-593/

Tiner, R.W. 1991. Recent changes in estuarine wetlands in the coterminous United States. Coastal Wetlands, Coastal Zone '91 Conference – American Society of Civil Engineers, Long Beach, CA. pp. 100–109.

Turner, R.E. and D.F. Boesch. 1988. Aquatic animal protection and wetland relationships: Insights gleaned following wetland loss or gain. In The Ecology and Management of Wetlands. Volume 1: Ecology of Wetlands. D.D. Hook, W.H. McKee, Jr., H.K. Smith, J. Gregory, V.G. Burrell, Jr., M.R. Devoe, R.E. Sojka, S. Gilbert, R. Banks, L.H. Stolzy, C. Brooks, T.D. Matthews, and T.H. Shear (eds.). Timber Press, Portland, OR.

U.S. Census Bureau. 2003. Population Datasets for Counties. Population Distribution Branch. U.S Census Bureau online information. http://www.census.gov/popest/datasets.html

U.S. Commission on Ocean Policy. Preliminary report, Governors' draft. 2004. Washington, D.C. 413 p. http://www.oceancommission.gov

U.S. Department of Agriculture (USDA). 1975. Soil taxonomy: A basic system of soil classification for making and interpreting soil surveys. Department of Agriculture. Soil Conservation Service, Soil Survey Staff, Agricultural Handbook 436, Washington, D.C. 754 p.

USDA. 1991. Hydric Soils of the United States. Soil Conservation Service, Miscellaneous Publication Number 1491, Washington, D.C.

U.S. Geological Survey. 1995. Louisiana Coastal Wetlands: A Resource At Risk. http://marine.usgs.gov/marine/fact-sheets/Wetlands/index.html

Watzin, M.C. and J.G. Gosselink. 1992. The fragile fringe: coastal wetlands of the continental United States. Louisiana Sea Grant College Program, Louisiana State University, Baton Rouge, LA. 16 p.

Williams, K., K.C. Ewel, R.P. Stumpf, F.E.Putz, and T.W. Workman. 1999. Sea-level rise and coastal forest retreat on the west coast of Florida, USA. Ecology, Vol. 80, No. 6, pp. 2045-2063.

APPENDIX:
DEFINITIONS OF HABITAT CATEGORIES

WETLANDS[5]

*I*n general terms, wetlands are lands where saturation with water is the dominant factor determining the nature of soil development and the types of plant and animal communities living in the soil and on its surface. The single feature that most wetlands share is soil or substrate that is at least periodically saturated with or covered by water. The water creates severe physiological problems for all plants and animals except those that are adapted for life in water or in saturated soil.

Wetlands are lands transitional between terrestrial and aquatic systems where the water table is usually at or near the surface or the land is covered by shallow water. For purposes of this classification wetlands must have one or more of the following three attributes: (1) at least periodically, the land supports predominantly hydrophytes[6], (2) the substrate is predominantly undrained hydric soil[7], and (3) the substrate is non-soil and is saturated with water or covered by shallow water at some time during the growing season of each year.

The term wetland includes a variety of areas that fall into one of five categories: (1) areas with hydrophytes and hydric soils, such as those commonly known as marshes, swamps, and bogs; (2) areas without hydrophytes but with hydric soils—for example, flats where drastic fluctuation in water level, wave action, turbidity, or high concentration of salts may prevent the growth of hydrophytes; (3) areas with hydrophytes but non-hydric soils, such as margins of impoundments or excavations where hydrophytes have become established but hydric soils have not yet developed; (4) areas without soils but with hydrophytes such as the seaweed covered portions of rocky shores; and (5) wetlands without soil and without hydrophytes, such as gravel beaches or rocky shores without vegetation.

MARINE SYSTEM – The marine system consists of the open ocean overlying the continental shelf and its associated high energy coastline. Marine habitats are exposed to the waves and currents of the open ocean. Salinity exceeds 30 parts per thousand, with little or no dilution except outside the mouths of estuaries. Shallow coastal indentations or bays without appreciable freshwater inflow and coasts with exposed rocky islands that provide the mainland with little or no shelter from wind and waves are also considered part of the Marine System because they generally support a typical marine biota.

ESTUARINE SYSTEM – The estuarine system consists of deepwater tidal habitats and adjacent tidal wetlands that are usually semi enclosed by land but have open, partly obstructed, or sporadic access to the open ocean and in which ocean water is at least occasionally diluted by freshwater runoff from the land. The salinity may be periodically increased above that of the open ocean by evaporation. Along some low energy coastlines there is appreciable dilution of sea water. Offshore areas with typical estuarine plants and animals, such as red mangroves (*Rhizophora mangle*) and eastern oysters (*Crassostrea virginica*), are also included in the Estuarine System.

---

[5] Adapted from Cowardin et al. 1979.
[6] The U.S. Fish and Wildlife Service has published the list of plant species that occur in wetlands of the United States (Reed 1988).
[7] U.S. Department of Agriculture has developed the list of hydric soils for the United States (U.S. Department of Agriculture 1991).

MARINE AND ESTUARINE SUBSYSTEMS

SUBTIDAL – The substrate is continuously submerged by marine or estuarine waters.

INTERTIDAL – The substrate is exposed and flooded by tides. Intertidal includes the splash zone of coastal waters.

PALUSTRINE SYSTEM – The palustrine (freshwater) system includes all nontidal wetlands dominated by trees, shrubs, persistent emergents, emergent mosses or lichens, farmed wetlands, and similar wetlands that occur in tidal areas where salinity due to ocean derived salts is below 0.5 parts per thousand. It also includes wetlands lacking such vegetation, but with all of the following four characteristics: (1) area less than 20 acres (8 ha); (2) an active wave formed or bedrock shoreline features are lacking; (3) water depth in the deepest part of a basin less than 6.6 feet (2 meters) at low water; and (4) salinity due to ocean derived salts less than 0.5 parts per thousand.

CLASSES

UNCONSOLIDATED BOTTOM – Unconsolidated bottom includes all wetlands with at least 25 percent cover of particles smaller than stones, and a vegetative cover less than 30 percent. Examples of unconsolidated substrates are: sand, mud, organic material, cobble gravel.

AQUATIC BED – Aquatic beds are dominated by plants that grow principally on or below the surface of the water for most of the growing season in most years. Examples include seagrass beds, pondweeds (*Potamogeton spp.*), wild celery (*Vallisneria americana*), waterweed (*Elodea spp.*), and duckweed (*Lemna spp.*).

ROCKY SHORE – Rocky shore includes wetland environments characterized by bedrock, stones, or boulders which singly or in combination have an areal cover of 75 percent or more and an areal vegetative coverage of less than 30 percent.

UNCONSOLIDATED SHORE – Unconsolidated shore includes all wetland habitats having two characteristics: (1) unconsolidated substrates with less than 75 percent areal cover of stones, boulders or bedrock and; (2) less than 30 percent areal cover of vegetation other than pioneering plants.

EMERGENT WETLAND – Emergent wetlands are characterized by erect, rooted, herbaceous hydrophytes, excluding mosses and lichens. This vegetation is present for most of the   growing season in most years. These wetlands are usually dominated by perennial plants.

SHRUB WETLAND – Shrub Wetlands include areas dominated by woody vegetation less than 20 feet (6 meters) tall. The species include true shrubs, young trees, and trees or shrubs that are small or stunted because of environmental conditions.

FORESTED WETLAND – Forested Wetlands are characterized by woody vegetation that is 20 feet (6 m) tall or more.

FARMED WETLAND – Farmed wetlands are wetlands that meet the Cowardin *et al.* definition where the soil surface has been mechanically or physically altered for production of crops, but where hydrophytes will become reestablished if farming is discontinued.

the substrate. As in wetlands, the dominant plants were hydrophytes; however, the substrates were considered nonsoil because the water is too deep to support emergent vegetation (U.S. Department of Agriculture 1975).

RIVERINE SYSTEM – The Riverine system includes deepwater habitats contained in a channel, with the exception of habitats with water containing ocean derived salts in excess of 0.5 parts per thousand. A channel is "an open conduit either naturally or artificially created which periodically or continuously contains moving water, or which forms a connecting link between two bodies of standing water" (Langbein and Iseri 1960).

LACUSTRINE SYSTEM – The lacustrine system includes deepwater habitats with all of the following characteristics: (1) situated in a topographic depression or a dammed river channel; (2) lacking trees, shrubs, persistent emergents, emergent mosses or lichens with greater than 30 percent coverage; (3) total area exceeds 20 acres (8 ha).

DEEPWATER HABITATS

Wetlands and deepwater habitats were defined separately because the term wetland does not include deep, permanent water bodies. For conducting status and trends studies, Riverine and Lacustrine were considered deepwater habitats. Elements of Marine or Estuarine systems can be wetland or deepwater. Palustrine includes only wetland habitats.

Deepwater habitats were permanently flooded land lying below the deepwater of wetlands. Deepwater habitats include environments where surface water is permanent and often deep, so that water, rather than air, is the principal medium in which the dominant organisms live, whether or not they were attached to

UPLANDS

AGRICULTURE[8] – Agricultural land may be defined broadly as land used primarily for production of food and fiber. Agricultural activity is evidenced by distinctive geometric field and road patterns on the landscape and the traces produced by livestock or mechanized equipment. Examples of agricultural land use include cropland and pasture; orchards, groves, vineyards, nurseries, cultivated lands, and ornamental horticultural areas including sod farms; confined feeding operations; and other agricultural land including livestock feed lots, farmsteads including houses, support structures (silos) and adjacent yards, barns, poultry sheds, etc.

---

[8] Adapted from Anderson *et al.* 1976.

Urban: Urban land is comprised of areas of intensive use in which much of the land is covered by structures (high building density). Urbanized areas are cities and towns that provide the goods and services needed to survive by modern day standards through a central business district. Services such as banking, medical and legal office buildings, supermarkets, and department stores make up the business center of a city. Commercial strip developments along main transportation routes, shopping centers, contiguous dense residential areas, industrial and commercial complexes, transportation, power and communication facilities, city parks, ball fields and golf courses can also be included in the urban category.

FORESTED PLANTATION: Forested plantations include areas of planted and managed forest stands. Planted pines, Christmas tree farms, clear cuts, and other managed forest stands, such as hardwood forestry are included in this category. Forested plantations can be identified by observing the following remote sensing indicators: 1) trees planted in rows or blocks; 2) forested blocks growing with uniform crown heights; and 3) logging activity and use patterns.

RURAL DEVELOPMENT: Rural developments occur in sparse rural and suburban settings outside distinct urban cities and towns. They are characterized by non-intensive land use and sparse building density. Typically, a rural development is a cross-roads community that has a corner gas station and a convenience store which are surrounded by sparse residential housing and agriculture. Scattered suburban communities located outside of a major urban center can also be included in this category as well as some industrial and commercial complexes; isolated transportation, power, and communication facilities; strip mines; quarries; and recreational areas such as golf courses, etc. Major highways through rural development areas are included in the rural development category.

OTHER LAND USE: Other Land Use is composed of uplands not characterized by the previous categories. Typically these lands would include native prairie; unmanaged or non-patterned upland forests and scrub lands; and barren land. Lands in transition may also fit into this category. Transitional lands are lands in transition from one land use to another. They generally occur in large acreage blocks of 40 acres (16 ha) or more and are characterized by the lack of any remote sensor information that would enable the interpreter to reliably predict future use. The transitional phase occurs when wetlands are drained, ditched, filled, leveled, or the vegetation has been removed and the area is temporarily bare.